SCREAMING ORGASMS GUARANTEED

SCREAMING ORGASMS GUARANTEED

SARAH TAYLOR

INSPIRED BOOKS

Published by Inspired Books

Manufactured in the United States of America

15 14 13 12 11 10 9 8 7 6 5 4 3 2 1

Library of Congress

ISBN: 978-0-9986819-3-1

Contents

Introduction

If you're ready for a sex life transformation and for scream-ing orgasms, this book is for you.

I am very excited to share this information with you.

I believe this content can do more than transform your or-gasms and sex life. It can revolutionize your relationship and life.

How? The information I'm about to reveal is proven to work. The specific techniques and application has helped couples finally have the powerful orgasms that help trans-form their sex lives and their relationship.

This strategy has helped couples literally reinvent their sex lives, achieve a bond they never thought possible, and even more.

The tools, techniques and strategies work, no matter who uses them.

During my years of counseling, one particular problem has been the most common and most frustrating to people: the orgasm. Especially for women.

If practiced, the content will guarantee that you will expe-rience fulfilling orgasms. Yes, screaming orgasms. Simultane-ous screaming orgasms. But the real goal is much bigger than just orgasms.

Yes, I will give you practical instructions about how to have loud, strong, freeing, and even life-changing orgasms.

But I want to do more than that, because the "more" is

when two people can really experience deep fulfillment in their sexual relationship and their overall relationship.

I want to give you practical, useful, helpful advice about romantic relationships and sex in general – and about orgasms that are an important and vital part of these relationships.

After years of counseling men, women, and couples, I've learned that the general advice about relationships and sex is just as important if not more important than the actual practical instructions about how to have screaming, simultaneous orgasms. Both are important, but one without the other would be incomplete.

If I just gave the instructions for orgasm, they may work, but you would not get the full benefits of the tips. It would be incomplete. And vice-versa.

So let's do it. And let's have fun. After all, that is what sex is all about.

And maybe we will grow some, too. Because that is also what sex is about.

And let's connect. Again, that's another aspect of sex......I think you get the point.

Sex is about much more than just orgasms and pleasure. Yes, I want to help you have screaming orgasms. But again, this book is about more than that.

Let's get started.

CHAPTER 1

The Orgasm

The Big O.

We want it. We need it.

Yet, for some people, especially during sex, it is elusive.

Many women even fake it.

There are several issues related to the orgasm that are challenging.

First, it's a very personal and private topic, and many people, if not most, are hesitant to discuss it personally and intimately.

Both sexes have challenges with the orgasm. For men, it might be premature ejaculation or erectile dysfunction.

For women, there are a variety of issues, with the main one being the major, crucial issue of not having an orgasm at all.

A challenge for many women is not having an orgasm during intercourse.

Another challenge for women is the whole issue of communication about orgasms, including the lack of orgasms, with their partner.

Whatever the problems, issues related to orgasms are rampant and detrimental to healthy, productive relationships and sex life.

In my counseling, the subject of orgasms has been the most difficult and exasperating for people. Part of this is that the orgasm issue is also one of the most difficult to talk about openly. As mentioned, and as we would all agree, it is highly personal and private.

Moreover, there is much misinformation and bad information out there, to the point of ridiculousness.

One of the purposes of this book is to shine a light on orgasms and provide practical, useful sex information you can use right away – and long term. If someone follows these instructions, they can and will have screaming orgasms, guaranteed.

I am referring to orgasms the way they are intended: real, genuine, satisfying, fulfilling, and enjoyable orgasms. They will experience the sexual release that we want, need and desire. Complete, total, real.

The Importance of the Orgasm

The subject of orgasms is incredibly important. Yet much of the "information" and public discourse available about it is misleading, confusing, superficial, bogus, and just plain false.

Even worse, in many places and sectors of society, orgasm is a taboo subject and is not freely and openly discussed. It is certainly not taught in schools, colleges, or religious institutions. (churches/synagogues.) We learn about all kinds of subjects in these places, yet one of the most important subjects- sex and orgasms- is almost completely ignored!

Schools, colleges and churches do not teach it. Parents usually do not discuss it with their children. So people of all ages search other places for answers. Often they cannot find any real, practical answers.

Yet the orgasm is an essential and crucial part of every romantic and loving relationship. It is absolutely vital to a good marriage and to reproduction, the two most fundamental human needs and desires. Yet the subject of orgasms is the least talked about and most misunderstood subject of just about every subject and topic out there.

I have seen sexual problems and the lack of orgasms break up relationships and marriages. And I have seen sexual fulfillment and real orgasms help save relationships and marriages.

So, these are some of the reasons I want to share this information with the public. Believe me, I myself am a private person and have no desire to become a "well-known author" or promote myself. I simply want to get useful information and advice to people. If I didn't have this information, I would hope someone would share it with me.

It is a tragedy that there is very little reliable, practical information about orgasms.

Where do we, especially young people, get our information? TV shows and movies certainly do not have reliable, credible information about the Big O. Magazines and websites for the most part provide basic information but do not go very deep. There are some good books about the subject, and a few will be mentioned in this book. But they are few and far between.

The worst is the porn industry. Their depiction of sex is so warped and twisted it is a wonder that anyone who watches porn (and there are millions who do) has any clue about real sex, orgasms, and sexual fulfillment.

CHAPTER 2

Sex is Fun!

Well, that's a given!

But I want to emphasize it, especially in a "sex manual," which has content that does require time, effort and perhaps changing some habits, so that we remember . . . sex is about fun, pleasure, enjoyment and so much more!

Our culture is so programmed for work and goals, we often apply that mentality to sex.

Sex is about a relationship, love, fun, enjoyment and more – not goals.

If someone incorporates the principles and techniques found in this book, they can and will have loud, releasing, full body, screaming orgasms! SO for short.

SOs may be the goal. But I want to share a secret: as I will discuss a little later, the most fulfilling sex and orgasms are when both partners are in love and are giving to their partner, not wanting to get or accomplish a goal. When this happens, the sky is the limit.

They will have the type of orgasm we are meant to have: a transformational, metamorphic experience that can revolutionize your sex life, your relationship and, believe it or not, even your daily life.

Wow! Is that really true?

Yes!

I do need to make a disclaimer. Someone needs to take the time and effort to implement various habits and develop the techniques to experience the transformation.

A Time and Place for Everything

Let me first state, sex is fun!

And much more!

Let's keep it that way!

It is exciting and adds the spice to life that we all want and need.

I want this book to be the same. So let's have fun as we go on this "transformational adventure" together.

As Woody Allen once said, "Sex is the most fun I've ever had without laughing."

Partners

Partners of course have different needs and desires when it comes to sex.

People experience a variety of moods and life phases that impact their sexual needs and desires.

Sometimes both partners want to just get right to intercourse. Sometimes one wants to and the other does not.

Perhaps one partner wants to go slower and enjoy teasing, foreplay and the exciting "preliminary activities," while the other is not in the mood for those.

Sometimes a partner wants to try some new positions, while the other partner does not.

And of course sometimes one partner is in the mood for sex and the other one is not.

This book presents numerous sexual techniques, including what I call The Technique, which is

A key is responding appropriately to your partners' needs and desires. A key is knowing when to use what techniques.

For those who simply want to find out The Technique and other related techniques, please go directly to page 37. Yes, the techniques can and will help you right away.

But remember, the best and most beneficial way to reap the benefits of this book is to read it all the way through and integrate the principles into your own life.

While sex is fun, it is also like a relationship. There is a need for continual communication, listening, trust, vulnerability, give and take, compromise, and more – the same qualities needed for a mature relationship.

But it's all worth it. A good sex life is stimulating and exhilarating, especially if it is approached and practiced according to certain principles.

CHAPTER 3

God Created Sex

I do not like over-spiritualizing anything. But the following point is important:

I believe God created sex.

I believe it is a divine gift.

Let me be honest and open. I am here to help. I would like to be your "book counselor," so to speak. I am on your side. I support you no matter what your spiritual beliefs are.

And this book will help you no matter what your spiritual beliefs are.

Your beliefs about a Higher Power/God is a personal, private matter. Even if we disagree, that's okay. We can agree to disagree.

We have many things in common. The fact that you are reading this book and exploring this topic is a big area of common ground we share. I myself am passionate about the subject of sexuality.

I am sure there are many things we have in common.

But even if we do not have all our spiritual beliefs in common, I again want to emphasize that these principles and this information can and will help you and apply to your relationships.

I will not push my beliefs on you or anyone. I just want to let you know what I believe about divinity and sex:

I believe God created sex.

Therefore, sex is a divine gift.

And here is a key: if two people realize and understand this truth, it will revolutionize their sex life and even their relationship.

Sex exists for many, many reasons! The following are just some of them:

1. Procreation/reproduction
2. The physical component of the union of two people
3. Pleasure
4. Fun and release
5. Health

We all know that sex is amazing.

But there is a sexual dimension that is so much better, higher and deeper than just the physical act of sex. It is the emotional, psychological, spiritual and metaphysical dimension of sex, one of the topics this book will explore and examine.

Beyond the Physical

An ideal is when a couple has spiritual and metaphysical sex.

They connect on the spiritual level.

A transformational truth is that human being's "dimensions" are all connected, including the physical, soulish, and spiritual.

Every dimension impacts the others. When a person is physically healthy, they are stronger in their mind, emotions and their spiritual self.

If someone eats healthy food and exercises regularly, it helps their mind and emotions. We think, work and feel better.

If someone does not eat proper meals, they literally do not think well and perhaps worse.

When someone is loving, a soulish emotion, it positively impacts their body and spirit.

And if someone has a great sex life, and has practical tools for having and enjoying sex and orgasms, it will greatly enhance and help their body, soul and spirit.

All areas of life are inter-connected. One thing affects another. The body affects the mind. The spirit affects the emotions. Food affects the will. Sex affects the spirit, the soul and the body. Are you following me?

This is why I am emphasizing a holistic approach to sex. It is a so important. It is a key. Your sex life can be many, many times more fun and fulfilling if it is approached holistically.

Sex is not just something that we have once a day, or three times a week, with the goal of having an orgasm and that's it. It is not something in its own compartment that we just get out for 20 minutes and then put back.

I want to help you make love all the time. I want to give you tools to help make your sex life all that it can be. And yes, I want to help you have screaming, simultaneous orgasms - guaranteed.

Ideally, it all goes together in one big package.

Two people can have sex only physically. They will likely not be fulfilled.

But if they connect spiritually and emotionally, with love for each other all the time, then this positive aspect of their relationship will of course greatly impact their sex life.

And a beautiful thing is the simplicity of it.

If a couple loves each other all the time, in the day-to-day experiences, in the practical and even simple areas (such as work, chores, errands, meals, hobbies, and more), they will naturally make love physically. And their physical, sexual bond will be greater and stronger.

Religions Impact on Our Culture's View of Sex

Throughout history, religion and certain cultures have severely damaged many peoples' views of and perspective about sex and orgasms.

These incorrect perspectives brainwashed people into thinking that sex was bad, shameful and only for procreation. These attitudes may have begun long ago and continued with the early religious movements such Puritanism and others.

In the United States, Americans are heirs to these traditions, which may not be as prevalent in other countries.

The truth is that God created sex. It is a wonderful gift of God. He said, "Be fruitful and multiply."

If someone is impacted by these very common beliefs, don't worry. You can change these patterns. It is helpful to be aware of it and make a conscious and concerted effort to be open-minded about sex. Books like this one are a good resource to help.

If a person believes that "sex is a sin," it of course severely limits their sexuality and potential for orgasms. An example is that it limits someone's ability to let go, which is a crucial aspect of achieving sexual release and sexual growth.

A goal of this book is to help you achieve a harmonious, proper and positive view of sex and sexuality, no matter what your training, environment, background and personality are.

CHAPTER 4

Stages of the Sexual Cycle

1. Foreplay
2. Stimulation
3. Dilation
4. Climax/Orgasm
5. Resolution

Dr. Lasse Hessel, the Danish inventor, author and doctor noted for such inventions as the Femi Dom and the Femi-X pill, is a leading sex expert. He presents this five-stage theory and believes that foreplay is more mental and emotional, while stimulation is physical, increasing blood flow to the genitals. The third stage increases blood flow so that the penis is erect and the scrotum swells, and the vagina and clitoris are enlarged.

Challenges

Goal-Oriented vs. Pleasure-Oriented Sex
If sex is viewed and approached as a goal-oriented event, with orgasm being the final goal, a person/couple limits his/

her/their ability to experience pleasure during the entire sexual experience.

There are two main approaches to sex: goal-oriented and pleasure-directed. A common problem that arises is when one partner, usually the male, takes the goal approach, while the other partner takes the pleasure approach. If they do not communicate properly, there can be problems.

The ideal approach is pleasure, in which every stage is an end in itself-- kissing, holding, oral sex, foreplay, and so forth. In this approach, there is no need to focus on a goal of orgasm. The best part is that usually every stage is enjoyed even more, including orgasm.

Variety of Sexual Response

One thing is sure: sexual response is different for every person. There are charts representing "sexual response cycles" for men and women. While these may be interesting and based on years of research, the reality is that every person's sexual cycle is different and unique.

In the same way, while every person can experience screaming orgasms, their actual SO's will be different and unique.

CHAPTER 5

The Purposes of Sex

Earlier, I listed some of the purposes of sex:

1. Procreation (making babies!)
2. The physical component of the union of two people
3. Pleasure
4. Fun and release

It is obvious that one of the main purposes of sex is procreation. It is how we have children.

Another purpose of sex is to be a sacred conduit or instrument for the union of two people becoming one.

This union is in the three dimensions we humans are able to dwell in: body, soul and spirit.

What does this mean- and why is this so important?

Ideally, a human can experience these three dimensions:

Body- Physical

Soul- Emotional/Psychological

Spirit- Spiritual

When two people have sex, that sexual act of making love is a conduit for them to experience a physical bond.

It is also a conduit for them to experience an emotional and psychological bond.

And, yes, you guessed it. It's also an instrument for them to experience deeper spiritual bond.

Remember earlier we discussed how all three parts of our being- body, soul and spirit- are interconnected? We are one being with three parts.

All three parts are 100%, completely connected and inter-twined.

Something done to the body affects the soul and spirit. And vice-versa.

Sex affects all three parts- body, soul and spirit.

Simply put, when two people have sex, it might look purely physical, but it will also affect their soul and their spirit.

Sex looks like a purely physical act, right? And some porno films make it out to be just that. But that is a very limited, shallow and superficial perspective about the wonderful and even sacred act of sex.

When someone physically has sex, it can be just a physical act- that is, two people just having intercourse for pure physical pleasure. But if it is, the two people are (simply explained) just receiving 33% of the potential benefits of sex. They are just experiencing the physical act of sex.

And they actually likely receive a lot less than 33%. Sex is a gift, and to experience the full benefits, it needs to be practiced according to certain principles, such as a monogamous relationship: one man with one woman in partnership.

There is so much more to sex and making love than just sex.

It is a tragedy if someone only experiences the physical dimension of sex.

CHAPTER 6

Why Women Fake Orgasms

It's a fact: many women fake having orgasms.

Women of all ages have never had one.

We should look at the male orgasm first.

Men and women would agree: it's easy for a man to orgasm. Their sex organs are outside their body. Men are (usually) easily aroused. Their orgasm has the visible sign of ejaculation. Men don't have to fake having the big O.

Furthermore, most often, men take the initiative in sex. They are assertive. They pursue. They lead. They are responsible for getting a woman pregnant. They have an orgasm. Their work is done (so to speak!)

But it's completely different for women regarding orgasms.

A major difference from men is of course that the female sex organs are not outside the body but within.

What are some relational, physiological reasons?

Some main reasons women fake orgasms:

First, she loves her man. She doesn't want to hurt his feelings or damage his ego. She wants him to be super-confident.

Second, she wants to be sexual and sensual, not perceived as something being wrong with her sexuality. She might even think it is her fault. After all, if he is having orgasms so easily, why would she have such a hard time? If he ever thought she was close to "frigid," she would be devastated. So she fakes.

Third, she does not know why she is not having one. She thinks it could be her fault. If she knew the answer, she might tell him. But even then, it is a delicate situation, as sex is a very personal area for both partners. She gets excited with foreplay. She is aroused. Her sex organs are tingling. She is ready. Then, the guy starts pumping in missionary, and soon thereafter, the "banging" actually hurts for sex organs. Her guy is getting great pleasure, while fairly soon, she wants it to end, so she fakes an orgasm.

This book's goal is to solve this dilemma.

More than that: I'm going to explain what to do to both arouse a woman and bring her to the most intense orgasm she's ever had, every time you make love.

One of the greatest results is that when she has this orgasm, the guy will be so excited that he will have an orgasm that surpasses any he's ever had, now that he knows how to truly pleasure her. And he will have a love for her he's never felt before.

And after the guy gives her this ultimate pleasure, she will be receiving what she wants and needs and loves, and she will only want him and no one else.

CHAPTER 7

How Men and Women Are Different

When it comes to loving and making love, men and women are wired in completely opposite ways. It is very important to understand and be aware of the following points, explained in more depth below:

1. Men love from the pelvic region up. Women love from the top down.

That is, men generally love from their genital area up. Women love from their head and mind down to their genital area.

2. Men are aroused by sight. Women are primarily aroused by touch. Women are also aroused mainly through the other taste and smell. Women are also aroused by sight.

3. Men think in 'compartments'; that is, every area has its own compartment (work, family, friends, play, health, etc.). Women think like a river- everything flows together.

One

We all know that men have a strong sex drive. The center of their sex drive is their genital area, their penis. A man gets aroused, he gets an erection. It's pretty simple.

For women it is more complex. They do not necessarily have a center of their sex drive. Their sex drive generally begins in their upper body area- their head and neck, their chest, their breasts. And then it moves down to their genital area.

Why is this important?

It is very important for both men and women to know these gender traits. It will help both a man and a woman to learn and understand how to make love much more effectively. And it is vital to understand this truth when learning the Big Secret Technique for screaming orgasms.

Men need to start their lovemaking experience "up top" with their woman. They should kiss their lover on the lips, face, cheeks, ears, neck and more.

Then they should begin to move down their body, to their chest, around their breasts, their shoulders, their arms. Then their breasts, their nipples, the entire breast and more. Then their stomach, their hips.......I think you get the point.

Two

Men are primarily aroused by sight.

Women are primarily aroused by touch.

Women are also aroused by smell and taste as well as by sight.

These facts are very important aspects of sex. If two people understand them, it will greatly enhance their sex life.

Men and sight. Again, it's pretty simple. Men get turned on by the sight of a woman. This is how men are wired. This is why men stare at women (lol). It is why men like "undressing" a woman in their mind. Men obviously like to see women in attire and accoutrements that reveal the female body: tight jeans, skimpy bikinis, lingerie, and more.

For women, arousal and attraction is different. Women are primarily turned on and aroused by touch; and secondarily by sight, taste and smell.

It is absolutely important for men to understand this. The lovemaking process begins with a man touching a woman lovingly, gently, sensuously. And starting from the top down.

And yes, women are also aroused by the other senses. This is why women love smells. Certain colognes and perfumes sexually stimulate a woman. This is why women love tastes- certain foods, sweets (chocolate), beverages (coffee) and more.

Three

Men's and women's minds work differently. This is very important to know and understand in relation to sex.

Men and women think and analyze differently. A brief explanation is that men think in "compartments"; that is, every area of life has its own compartment. Women think like a river: everything flows together.

The different 'areas of life' might be: family, marriage, friends, work, hobbies, health, religion and so on. Some areas might have a sub-areas, such as the friend area: best friends, friends, acquaintances, work friends, etc.

For men, every one of these areas is compartmentalized and dealt with on its own. A man works, and his work and career is its own entity. He deals with work on its own separate from the other areas. He deals with every area on its own.

It is completely different for a woman. All the areas flow together- work and family and friends and hobbies and fun and health and spiritual beliefs.......and sex.

This truth is very important to understand. If a man who is in a romantic relationship with a woman can understand this and act accordingly, their sexual relationship will be so much better and stronger and deeper.

For a woman, every area affects every other area. Work affects friends. Health affects spiritual. Marriage affects hobbies. And on and on. All the areas affect her sex life. And her sex life affects all the other areas.

For example, if a woman has peace, harmony and serenity in the various areas of her life (the list above), her sex life is much more likely to be full of peace and harmony.

When a man understands this, it can greatly enhance a couple's sex life. When he realizes that she thinks differently in her approach to sex and to all areas of life, he will understand that the way he treats her during the day- in normal activities- directly affects their sex life.

If a woman feels nurtured and loved in areas such as work, friendships, family, and hobbies, she will be more responsive and fulfilled in sex. So, a man may not want to attend that family gathering or be involved with his partner's hobby, but it is important that he does these things. For a woman, all areas are part of the same river, flowing together in one direction.

With a man, he just wants to have great sex and that's it. Sex is in its own "compartment," separate from everything else. He needs to realize how a woman thinks and feels.

CHAPTER 8

Sex with Love

Sex is a vital part of a person's overall health and wellness. But not just sex. A key is . . . sex with love.

So, the very first component of health and wellness is of course love.

Sex with love is fulfilling physically, emotionally and mentally. Moreover, it helps two partners bond in those ways as well.

Love is Powerful

Love is powerful – for us and for those we love.

We all have the capacity for it, but the negative forces of life often keep us from loving and being loved. We might be worried, fearful, hurt, scarred, depressed or similar emotions.

I do not want to "preach" or sound self-righteous. Most likely know how important love is.

But when it comes to sex, because sex itself is so amazing, we often forget that the greatest and most beneficial sex is . . . sex with love.

Sex without love is an exercise.

Love: Listen, Overlook, Value, Encourage

When we give and receive love, it helps US!

If someone is self-interested and wants the best for themselves, they will love! That love will come back to them.

So, just a little "pep talk." Practice love. Love yourself and others – and especially your partner. Let go of the negative and embrace the positive – and especially love. When two partners love each other, they can make love all the time.

Giving and Receiving

An aspect of love is giving, to the right people, to family and friends.

And the following is another powerful aspect of sex: in a sexual relationship, when both partners love and are giving 100% to their partner in sex, they are also receiving 100%! Both partners are giving fully and receiving fully. How cool is that!

CHAPTER 9

Foreplay

Foreplay is by far the most underrated aspect of sex.

Making love actually begins before foreplay, with two partners giving affection and more.

Most know that foreplay builds arousal in both partners. It is especially important for the woman, to get her sex organs ready for intercourse.

A key is teasing.

This short chapter's specific content about teasing is vital to incorporating The Technique into your sex life.

If you have not, just try it.

For the guy: early in foreplay, gently touch her skin anywhere – her back, arms, legs, it can be anywhere.

The key is gentle, light, soft and easy. Go slow. Don't rush it. Take at least a minute or two in an area other than her breasts.

You're creating desire and arousal. She wants something else very much. What? She wants you to go to her breasts. You're not going there just yet.

Be deliberate. Tease her. Then go to her breasts but not her nipples yet. Gently touch the skin on her breasts for a minute or two before going to her nipples.

Then, softly, gently go to her nipples. Barely touch them.

What is this going? It is highly arousing her.

You are taking the lead, which is also a big turn-on.

You are creating desire. The more you create it, the more she wants you to satisfy it.

You're also creating a massive desire within her sex organs.

When she's ready, and you're ready with an aroused and hard penis, you're both ready for The Technique.

CHAPTER 10

The Technique

The best technique was saved for last . . .

Before the actual technique is put into action, the steps leading up to it need to part of the whole package in order to experience screaming orgasms. It is important to go through the whole progression, not just jump right into The Technique.

And there are techniques along the way that can heighten pleasure and the orgasms.

I want to emphasize that a lover needs to be creative and original. The practical steps are important, but they are just general guidelines to follow, not a "formula" or exact recipe. Follow your intuition and gut instinct.

If the steps are "covered" and experienced, then The Technique is a formula that works. At some point it could become you and your lover's primary "repertoire." It might work the very first time you use it. It may take a few tries and some practice. If the steps in this book are followed, it will work.

The general steps are: flirting, foreplay and building arousal.

Drum roll please....................

Okay, you have flirted and shown affection for your lover away from foreplay and sex.

You have engaged in effective foreplay for an appropriate amount of time.

Now you are getting close to beginning The Technique (TT).

Remember, the stages and steps leading up to TT flow together and become one big stage and step. So, there may not be a "moment" when you begin TT the technique. The start and stop times blur, and it's better this way.

Men: as you transition from foreplay to TT, build arousal through teasing. As clothes come off, preferably slowly, there are countless ways to proceed.

You might kiss your lover's face, neck and other areas and then move down toward her breasts, but then move away before you actually get to her breasts. Go to another place nearby- shoulders, near her shoulders, upper arms, etc. Then back toward his breasts.

Perhaps do this a number of times, getting closer to her nipples every time. Perhaps move to her stomach, sides, rib cage and lower back. Go back to her breasts, this time closer to her nipples, but do not touch them yet. This will tease her to new heights. She may be ready to explode before you even go below the waist.

At the right time, you might touch her areola and nipples, lightly and gently at first, starting outside and moving in. Go with the flow and use your intuition.

The Technique

Position: woman is lying down on a bed with legs spread. Man is on his knees, kneeling before her genital area (I like that: kneeling, almost in worship.....lol)

Men: take your erect penis in your hand. With the head of your penis, begin to stimulate her vaginal lips, clitoral hood, and clitoris and the areas around them.

Stimulate her clitoris with your penis head, rhythmically going back and forth, flicking it at different speeds and tempos. Go around and around the clitoris, clockwise and counterclockwise. You will soon find out what specific motions and speeds she loves and desires.

Slowly, deliberately run your penis' head around the highly sensitive and erogenous areas of the genital area. Be creative. Notice the sensations and her reactions.

Enjoy it and let her enjoy it. Do it slowly and patiently. Have fun (Do I need to remind you of that?)

Keep eye contact during appropriate times during this stage. Perhaps speak sensuously and softly to her.

At the appropriate time, penetrate her ever so slightly. But only a little. Go back to the lips and clit.

By this time, she likely will be moaning and groaning with pleasure.

Keep going. Perhaps go back to licking and caressing her inner thighs and nearby zones. Again, go with your intuition. Be creative. Mix it up. Do something different every time.

Then go back to the lips and clit. Maybe go back to oral stimulation. Go back to penis' head stimulation. Now penetrate a little deeper. Just a little deeper this time.

Tantalize and tease her. She may be begging you to penetrate now.

Some couples at some point just start penetration. And the man may orgasm right away, as both partners are so sexually charged. This what making love is all about. It might be similar, it might be different. But it's always exciting.

There are many ways you can go with this.

Key: as the man builds strong arousal in his partner, she will begin getting close to a screaming orgasm.

Both partners will know when it is close.

There is an initial stage of 3-4 seconds before orgasm called "orgasmic inevitability" (OI) when a person knows they are headed for the Big O.

When two lovers get in tune with their sexual energy, a man will be able to tell when his lover is in this very brief pre-Big O stage.

Her face and body will tighten up right before that massive release of voice, noise and energy during a screaming orgasm. She may gasp in a very different and unique way- the sign she is at OI.

When she arrives at the SO, there are many options for how to experience it.

During a screaming orgasm, with the inherent physical and emotional release, both a woman and a man may scream with rhythmic yells (utterances) that vary in pitch and tone for anywhere from seven to 12 seconds. They will feel suspended in time. They will enter into another realm and dimension- the orgasmic dimension- that tops every other feeling and sensation and leaves them speechless.

It is sexually, physically, and emotionally fulfilling. Yet, there is even something more fulfilling, explained below.

Their body will experience a complete release of tension and even pain.

Their screams might be "oh-oh-ohs" or similar frenzied gasps and vocals.

They may continue on with "multiples," multiple orgasms of two or more, with short intervals between. They key is to let them happen naturally. Several factors impact whether or not a couple experiences multiples, such as sexual chemistry, overall health (another reason to pursue a healthy lifestyle), and genetics.

Everyone's orgasmic scream is unique.

A woman's orgasmic screams will usually be short, fast, high-pitched utterances in very quick succession. A man's screams will be similar but deeper in pitch and tone.

Now, the most sexually fulfilling thing.

Guys experience OI also. If the guy can delay his orgasm and release it in tune with his partner, the couple can experience a simultaneous orgasm (simo). The more a couple practices and develops their sexual chemistry, the more likely they will be able to experience simos.

I have counseled couples who went from never having orgasms to have simos every night- long, deep, pleasurable simos that

CHAPTER 11

Boundaries

The concept of boundaries may not seem relevant to a discussion or manual about sex. However, it is very important and even vital.

Proper boundaries can revolutionize your relationships-and your sex life. They are so necessary to a good sex life that I often counsel people about boundaries first before getting into the whole sexual area (though the reality is that "the sexual realm" includes everything about our relationship . . . this is a key to this book and message.) Boundaries are the necessary foundation needed for healthy relationships and a healthy sex life.

What are boundaries? They are personal "property lines" that distinguish what is your emotional and personal property and what belongs to others.

Boundaries help define us and protect us. They let the good in- and keep the bad out. They can be one of the most helpful tools to develop love, responsibility, and freedom.

It is extremely important to develop and nurture proper sexual boundaries in relationships, both a current relationship and past relationships. As Cloud and Townsend point out in their Boundaries series, there are seven qualities necessary for a healthy relationship:

Honesty
Communication
Listening
Trust
Vulnerability
Assertiveness
Self-sacrifice

These seven keys apply to sex too. Each of us need to develop and practice these qualities in order to have a healthy sexual relationship. They are the foundation; a good sex life is the result.

There are numerous examples of "healthy boundaries in action." We need to let our partner know how far we want to go physically and sexually. Communication is vital. We need to confront issues and problems- and take responsibility for them, proactively and not reactively. Assertiveness.

We need to allow time or space between us and our partner as a consequence for certain actions. We should have supportive friends to help us navigate our relationship.

When both partners give (including during sex), they move into realms of true fulfillment. Self-sacrifice.

Boundaries provide freedom and choices. They help define and protect priceless aspects of your being: your love, emotions, values, behaviors, and attitudes.

When someone possesses boundaries, they are more likely to have a healthy sex life and avoid the extreme emotional baggage and damage from dysfunctional sexual relationships (one-night stands; unwanted sexual activity; STDs, etc.)

Moreover, in an era when most people have multiple sex partners, both in the past and future, boundaries help us keep our "sanity" when we move into a new sexual relationship. If we maintain boundaries from the get-go, we are more likely to have fulfilling sexual relationships- and we are more likely to be able to move on when a relationship ends.

CHAPTER 12

Health and Wellness

Good news! The content and principles in this chapter will enhance your sex life!

If practiced, this information can improve your entire life! It can make you feel and look better and younger. . . and make your sex life better!

Sometimes we think that anything health-related is a "chore." In reality, it is fun and reaps great benefits, including in our sex life.

Keys to Health and Well-Being

A health guru believes there are at least 15 things necessary for complete health. The list is by no means comprehensive, but it is certainly something worth considering. The list:

1. Proper relationship with God
2. Proper relationship with all people
3. Harmonious family relationships
4. Harmonious friendships with like-minded people
5. A vocation for subsistence (paying the bills) and providing something beneficial to the community

6. Hobbies to provide balance
7. A positive attitude
8. A diet full of fresh, whole foods
9. Regular exercise
10. Proper body temperature
11. Fresh air (open windows often in your house)
12. Fresh water
13. Sufficient sleep
14. Laughter with friends
15. Sexual release

Holistic Approach to Diet and Exercise

An orgasm book would be incomplete if it only dealt with sex techniques. I want to pass along info about diet, exercise and health that greatly impact sex and orgasms.

The area of health and well-being might be one of the most important factors impacting sex and orgasms.

And there is so much more than just diet and exercise that contributes to and impacts a person's health and well-being.

Some simple tips have helped numerous clients and friends lift their sex life to higher levels.

Endorphins

Let's start with something often neglected but SO important: endorphins.

Endorphins are something that the body produces naturally that act as natural stimulants. They actually resemble drugs (opiates) in their ability to produce a feeling of well-being and analgesia (pain killers).

Simply put, endorphins are an incredible mechanism in the body for health and wellness – and for helping improve a person's sex life.

Endorphins are released in a variety of ways, especially during: exercise, eating, laughing, smiling, excitement, listening to pleasurable music, experiencing nature, pain, love, sex and orgasm.

I encourage everyone I counsel to do as many things as possible to release endorphins!! Make it a priority- and have fun and enjoy it, because it is fun.

There are many, many ways to release endorphins, and they are not just limited to the list above. If there is something that causes you excitement, it will release endorphins. The releasers are different for everyone.

Now, I also encourage people to keep everything in perspective and practice restraint and moderation. There are obviously things that might release endorphins that are not beneficial, and we can overdo it.

But it is true that many people do not understand endorphins and therefore do not get the benefits of them.

Sex and orgasm are probably the two most endorphin-releasing activities. Therefore, they are highly effective tools for health and well-being. More on this later.

Diet

Do what works for you.

If it's not working, I have some practical tips that can help. Even if it is working, these tips can help.

We all want to be physically fit and proportionate, right? We all want and need to be in good physical shape.

When someone is height/weight proportionate (that is, no more than five pounds overweight), their sex life and their orgasms are much better.

Fact: For humans, there are two main types of eaters. Some

people prefer a diet of primarily meats/proteins. Other people prefer vegetables/fruits/grains/carbs.

Studies show that a person's blood type actually determines what they prefer and crave. There are other factors, too, such as environment (if someone if from a meat-eating region, they may prefer meats because they are used to it.)

For your food cravings, go with your gut instinct, your heart instinct (gut- no pun intended.) If you love meat, go for it. If you love grains and breads and starches, have at it.

Within this context, there are some important principles to be aware of.

Some of the best diet advice I have received is below:

1. If it has a label on it, don't eat it.

2. Anytime food has been tampered with and altered, that food likely will alter our body mechanisms designed to keep us fit and healthy. Moral: don't eat altered food. Try to eat food in its natural state, such as whole foods.

3. Whole foods would be straight up foods just like they come in nature: vegetables, fruits, grains, breads, starches (rice, pasta, potatoes, etc), legumes, nuts, etc. It is best to eat them without any other ingredients (such as sugar, preservatives, etc.)

4. Everything you eat can and should taste great!! Enjoy it. If it is not something you like and look forward to eating, do not eat it.

5. A person can eat great-tasting, healthy food EVERY MEAL if they want. And it can done with the same budget as any other diet. No need to go overboard and shop at expensive health food stores. Just purchase whole foods.

6. A person can also find healthy, great-tasting sweets, snacks and desserts at most major grocery stores in the health food section (snacks, bars, cereals, candy, etc, etc.)

7. Fruit is one of the healthiest foods in the world. Always

eat fruit on an empty stomach. Fruit is digested in the intestines and not the stomach. (This is why many people get indigestion, etc.) Try to eat fruit early in the day.

8. Eat in moderation. Do not overeat. Eat to live; do not live to eat.

9. Drink eight glasses of purified water every day (distilled is the best; avoid tap and spring water.) Drink a glass of water 10 minutes before a meal (or at least some water).

10. Do not mix meat and starches (yes, Americans do this every meal. That is one of the reasons Americans are so unhealthy, obese and sick!!)

11. Animal products are generally not healthy. This includes: meats and dairy products (milk, cheese, ice cream, etc.)

12. Avoid junk food.

13. Your taste buds and your body cravings change (in about 21 days) depending on the food you eat. If you eat healthy food, within a few weeks your body will only crave the healthy food and not the unhealthy food.

14. Enjoy your food!

Exercise

The benefits of exercise are numerous and amazing. Among many benefits, exercise: controls weight; combats disease and reduces chance of disease; improves mood; improves psychological well-being; boosts energy; promotes better sleep; reduces depression and anxiety; improves your sex life; and numerous other advantages.

Some people like a gym, others like the outdoors. Some like indie workouts, some like a group or class.

Some people run or cycle. Some like weights. Some like yoga or pilates.

Try to work out 3 to 5 times per week with at least 2-3 30 minute cardio work outs per week. The key with cardio is to get your heart rate accelerated.

If you cannot get a full workout in, at least do something. Take a walk, do push-ups and sit-ups, etc. Get a small trampoline and do resistant rebounding, a very effective, economical workout.

Yoga is a fantastic form of exercise. It can help overcome a host of physical problems and challenges.

Some Secrets about Health

I want to share three "insider" tips about health, gained after years and years of counseling, that I think will truly help anyone interested in being healthy. In addition, this information also reveals why orgasms are so healthy and good for the human body.

The Body Works Like a Circuit

A very respected, longtime physical therapist once explained to me that the human body works like a circuit. There are many circuits in the body, but the absolute main ones are: the neck; the lower back; and the ankles.

If someone can keep these three parts of their body generally healthy, they themselves can stay healthy a long, long time and live a long life.

If any of these three parts "loses" it's health, watch out! It could mean trouble in the rest of the body.

From a practical perspective, the three main circuits make sense: they are the top and bottom of the critically-important spine; and the ankles and feet are the foundation of the entire body.

The flow of spinal fluid, discussed below, is related to these circuits.

Orgasms are very healthy, as they allow the circuits to release and get free from pain, stiffness, and blockages.

CHAPTER 13

Body Image

A healthy, positive body image is a key to great sex. Remember, every person on the earth is beautiful and attractive. In fact, every person is way more than that. You are priceless.

In our society today, it is very difficult to have a positive view of our body. The media and people in general have a warped view of what a "beautiful," "attractive," and "sexy" person looks like. Remember, their "definition" is just their idea. It does not make it right.

What is true "beauty"? What body type is "attractive"? I challenge all my clients to set their own standards for what is beautiful, attractive, and sexy.

True beauty comes from within. The saying, 'beauty is only skin deep,' is true. And sexuality is much deeper. In terms of sex and sexuality, a person's attitude, approach, and perspective regarding sex is actually what is truly sexy.

Studies show that around 90% of women and 70% of men are unhappy with something about their appearance.

A healthy body-image is the foundation and starting place for your sexuality. It's important to accept and love your body—and yourself—in order to develop a healthy sex life.

First, set your own standards for what is attractive and beautiful. This is absolutely important. This same principle applies to everything: success, happiness, fulfillment, and so forth. This process is freeing and fun. It's liberating.

Regarding our actual body, everyone has a unique body type with certain specific characteristics. Generally speaking, I've seen individuals gain a very healthy body-image when they embrace their uniqueness and unique characteristics. It might be height, weight, facial features, hair type, body type, breast size, legs, anything. They accept, embrace, and enjoy their unique features as a beautiful person.

It's healthy to follow the wise saying: "God grant me the serenity to accept the things I cannot change, the courage to change the things I can, and the wisdom to know the difference."

It's a very healthy process. A person accepts their body. After consideration, they might endeavor to change aspects of their body they can change (weight is a prime example).

But there is something even more important in this equation related to the body. Call the "intangibles." I see this time and time again in my practice.

Specific Cases

Cindy is a knockout beauty. For several years, she has dated a very successful guy named Steve, who is widely considered a "hunk." Overall things are going well. But there just seems to be something missing in their sex life. To make a long story short, their lack of connection sexually has almost threatened to break up their relationship.

Julie is a hard-working professional and is considered "normal-looking" but without "model" good looks. She's dating Bill, and overall things are fine. While she may not be a "looker," Julie's sex life sizzles, and both she and Steve are very fulfilled sexually. Through the years, Julie has developed into a great lover.

What pattern is presented here? Many times I have seen it, though it is not always the case. Oftentimes, "beautiful" people have not had to develop their "lover" skills—they get by on their looks.

The "average-looking" people have had to develop their sexual and love-making skills, since they do not rely on looks. They make up for it by becoming good and oftentimes great lovers.

What is my point? The "intangibles" related to our sexuality, and to our body-image, are just as if not more important than our actual "looks." I am referring to such things as our personality, attitude, demeanor, and perspective about sex. It's many, many things related to our sexuality. They are very difficult to describe; they're intangible.

It's in a good lover's body language, eyes, and voice. It's their passion and approach, their attitude and reactions to their partner. It's how they interact and response, how they talk and listen. It almost cannot be taught, but then again, someone can develop into a good lover.

A good lover enjoys, likes, and flows with the entire love-making process, from eye contact all the way to climax and cuddling. Their body language is positive and uplifting. They make their partner feel special, wanted, and desired. They know how to use their voice and words to create desire and passion. It's an aura that "oozes" and "flows forth" from a good lover. Their demeanor and disposition is so "loud" it overshadows their looks.

These are just some examples. But the main point here is that these intangibles are perhaps more important than looks. It takes effort, time, and trial and error to develop into a good lover. It takes work. You have to change. It can be done, don't worry about that.

Then begin a new process of getting to know yourself and your beauty – your pricelessness.

Get in touch with your body. Appreciate it. Accept what you cannot change. And yes, it's okay and encouraged to have a plan to change things you are able to change and want to change.

Sic Focus on the positives about your body. It helps to write down what you like – and what you'd like to work on. Perhaps you want to get in better physical shape. Maybe lose a few pounds. Maybe you want to have better posture. Use less or more makeup. Live a more balanced life. Get more sleep. Write you're your general ideas and goals. Enjoy the process. Don't treat it like a "job." This is a privilege: you are beautiful, and you are becoming more beautiful every day.

All of this will allow you to become more free and less inhibited in bed.

Nakedness

It's important and fun to get very comfortable with your nakedness. A good lover is very happy being naked with someone else – and doing more than just being naked. The following are some basic exercises to help in this process:

1. Spend time on a daily or weekly basis (whatever you feel is right for you) walking in your bedroom and even in your home naked. (Whatever is appropriate; if there are others in the home, it might be just in your bedroom.)

Really get into it. Enjoy it. Enjoy how it feels to be in your natural state, free from clothing but, in a deeper sense, free from restrictions.

Maybe do some yoga and stretching. Breath. Reflect. Pray/ take moment of silence.

Some people do this after taking a shower as a matter of health and well-being. It lets the body "air out," detox, and breath. It's not as healthy to have layers of clothes on all the time. Our bodies to do not get a chance to "live" and breath as much.

Feeling Sexy

Sexiness comes from within. Someone is sexy when they know they are sexy and have confidence and are comfortable in their bodies. Usually, whether man or woman, they have a quiet confidence. Feeling sexy is not about looks but rather about an inward confidence and feeling.

In a relationship, sexiness is enhanced when the two partners openly communicate about wants, needs and desires. An example is letting your partner know what you like, what excites you and attracts you.

CHAPTER 14

The Senses

The five senses are another passageway and conduit to a better sex life and to screaming orgasms.

Sight

As mentioned, men are aroused by sight. The visual of an attractive woman drives men wild. It's simple but true. Ladies, always be aware of this powerful truth.

Ever wonder why men stare at women? Ever wonder why they like skin flicks, porn, women in bikinis and all that type of stuff? Men are visual. That is why men as consumers (and thus women as well) are bombarded with visuals of "attractive" women: television, movies, magazines, advertisements, billboards, posters . . . it never ends. The corporate world knows what drives men wild: visual images of women.

So, ladies, learn from this and take note. Whether you are out of or in a relationship, the way you look and take care of yourself makes a big difference in your relationships and in your sex life.

But I am referring to much more than just "looks." I am

writing about (and I counsel my clients about this) . . . you, the entire person. It's much more than just the physical. I am referring to the intangibles. Just a few examples are: energy, confidence, poise, self-assurance, spirit, cheerfulness. It is the intangible characteristics that are truly beautiful to others. Please see the section on body language on page   .

It is certainly important to look your best physically. I am all for that. But true beauty – and beauty that can be a vital part of a great sex life – is so much more. It's an inner and outer beauty.

Yes, I am also referring to how you take care of yourself. Learn more about this in the health and well-being section on page   .

I believe that everyone on earth is beautiful. It's not the way you were made that matters; it's what you do with it. All women and all men are beautiful. In fact, they are more than just beautiful. They are priceless.

Understatement

In case you do not know this about me yet, I believe in the power of understatement. I believe that sometimes more is less and less is more.

As mentioned earlier, modern media/corporate entities bombard with a message, and usually it is one of "excess and overkill" related to what is accepted as "beautiful" and "fulfilling." I encourage my clients to find out what he or she thinks is beautiful and pursue that – not what the "world" tells us.

Sometimes clients find out that it's the simple things that are the most fulfilling. And it is amazing how "self-discovery" like this can help transform someone's sex life.

I'll give you an example. Mindy seemed to have it all. She had a great career, an ambitious and successful husband, and very nice material things (house, car, vacation home.) But she was very unhappy (she told me this privately). I encouraged her to enter a season of self-discovery and find out the things she truly enjoyed and which might give her fulfillment- not what her family or friends or the world believes bring happiness.

She soon realized it was the very simple things that brought her the most joy. Time spent with a good friend. Helping someone in need, anonymously. Spending a long weekend volunteering for a cause instead taking a beach trip.

She found out what really made her tick, and this "energy" revitalized her in numerous ways, including her sex life. It amazed her when this inner fulfillment helped her and her husband's sex life. But I have seen this happen over and over again.

Moderation, Variety, and a Season

The world teaches "excess." I feel and believe the more effective principles involve moderation, variety, and similar credos.

The world wants you to buy and use their products. They push a look of "beauty" that apparently will bring happiness. But what truly causes someone to be happy? I encourage you to pursue self-discovery.

In the meantime, the principles of moderation and a "season for everything" actually can help someone's sex life. Everything in moderation. There is a season for everything under the sun.

Regarding looking nice: I'm all for it. I encourage you and all my clients to look their best and pursue a lifestyle of health and well-being.

But there is a time and place for everything. For women,

there is a time for dressing up and a time for dressing down. A time for make-up and perfume and a time for the au naturale look; that is, no make-up, no perfume, simple clothes, etc. It all depends on the occasion. Same thing for men.

I think we should all look our best. And women especially, since men are so wired for the visual. But I encourage women not to go overboard. Try modesty on for size. Go out sometimes without make-up and without dazzling clothes. You'll be surprised at how your man- and men in general- will respond.

Touch

Women are aroused primarily by touch and secondarily by taste, sight and hearing. Men, this very important to know and understand.

The understanding of how a woman is wired is absolutely essential to great love-making and orgasms.

Touch includes many aspects of contact that some men do not realize. It is not just touching a woman with your hands. It is so much more.

Just some examples of touch include: closeness, holding hands, walking arm in arm, hugging, embracing, kissing, sitting/reclining next to each other, massage and more.

Touching is something a man and woman can do throughout a typical day to stay connected and build arousal. A man in tune with this can help elevate his and his lover's attracting and sexual energy.

Tip: Ideally, a couple touches throughout the day when they are together. It happens naturally, easily and spontaneously. It becomes second nature, a habit, which makes it even more natural. Foreplay is a natural extension of this ongoing touching.

Sometimes the touching itself will lead to foreplay and sex. Other times, it will not. It all depends on the situation.

Taste

Our sense of taste definitely affects our sensuality and potential for orgasms. Remember that women are aroused by taste. This is why women love sweets, beverages and similar items.

Remember the truth: everything is inter-connected. The same is true for the senses. The sense of taste and smell are connected. When someone smells something appetizing, their mouth may water with a desire to taste it. Conversely, if someone smells something bad, they get a bad taste in their mouth. If you like how your partner smells, it increases your desire to kiss, fondle and taste them.

Tip: Always try to smell good! Maintain proper personal and oral hygiene. I encourage clients to maintain this naturally and not try to cover up smells with perfume, cologne or fragrances. Find out what your lover likes and do that.

Moreover, what we do with our mouth has a two-pronged effect of stimulating our sense of taste and our sense of touch. Think about it: when we eat, our sense of touch is very involved. We prepare and handle food with our hands. We eat with our lips, tongue and mouth. Touch is involved during the entire process.

The same is true with our sexuality. We touch, taste, lick and suck our lover, just like we do with food. To be blunt, a lover may suck and lick their partner all over their body, just like with food- ice cream cones, lollipops, beverages and more.

Certain foods and beverages are known to be sensuous. Some of them include: sushi, oysters, wine, espresso, desserts, whipped cream, nuts, virtually all the fruits, figs, dates and more. Some herbs known to be sensuous are: ginger, cayenne and basil.

Smell

Our sense of smell is very important to us and to our sexuality. Studies have shown that smell strongly impacts who we fall in love with – and other important aspects of the romantic experience.

Smells impact us. They are a powerful trigger of memories. Aromatherapy is an entire field of alternative medicine that deals with the phenomenon of how smells impact our mind, mood, and health.

We all have certain smells we love and certain smells we literally despise. Much of this is based on the memory the smell triggers.

Women generally have a more keen sense of smell than men. Research has shown that when women are in the presence of a preferred scent, they project positive feelings which leads to increased attraction. It's no wonder women enjoy numerous aromas and take time to make them a part of their life: foods, fragrances, perfumes, oils, aroma jars, room spray, scented candles and more.

Our sense of smell strongly impacts our sexuality. An inability to smell has been associated with a decreased interest in sex.

Certain smells act as strong aphrodisiacs, or sexual stimulants. For women, some of these smells include: vanilla, peppermint, musk, patchouli, ylang ylang and jasmine.

For men, examples of sexually stimulating smells are: cinnamon buns, doughnuts, licorice, pumpkin pie, orange, lavender, buttered popcorn, and cheese pizza. Other sexy smells are: frankincense, lime, rose, and ginger.

Back to the choice of mate/smell connection.

Have you ever noticed that people smell a certain way? Like fingerprints, every person has an "odor print." Humans have a region of genes known as the major histocompatibility complex (MHC). Women prefer men whose MHC scent is different from their own.

One explanation of this phenomenon is that "opposite immune systems" are attracted to each other, which is Nature's way of ensuring healthy offspring.

Tip: Find out the smells that your lover craves and enjoys, and incorporate them into your romance. Health food stores will have all the aromas and devices needed to diffuse them.

There have even been studies which reveal that ovulating women prefer the smell of dominant men, such as men who exhibit dominance and therefore stronger genes.

Sound

Noise affects us and our psyche, either positively or negatively, in important and vital ways. Study after study reveals this. In the same way, noise and music affect our sexuality in profound and dramatic ways. As with everything, noise affects us holistically, affecting our entire being.

First, the positive. Picture a relaxing evening in your cozy, quiet den, without any distractions. Smooth jazz music is playing in the background, including some sexy saxophone songs. A quiet fountain is running that sounds like a relaxing stream flowing nearby. You and your lover talk quietly, with affirmations and positive words, sometimes in normal tone, sometimes in a whisper.

You engage in some simple sexy pillow talk (see page   for the section on pillow talk and its importance). You talk affectionately and sincerely, lifting each other up, heightening the situation, and having fun. The words and perhaps more importantly the sound of your voice heightens your mood, your senses, and your sexual vibrancy. The words are important, yes. But the tone and sound of your voice is just as important if not more so. It's not just what you say; it's how and when and why you say it and how you feel when you say it.

The setting is perfect for love-making.

This situation is easy and simply- and natural. Don't think it is only for those "chosen" few lovers who are "born to be great lovers." It's simply a matter of putting forth some effort and getting the environment right, and perhaps changing some of your habits related to your home, your communication, your priorities and so forth. Sometimes it's just a matter of slowing down, living in the moment, living a balanced life (please see section on Balance, page   ).

Noise and music can literally affect our overall health and sex life directly. Noise affects our being. It can slow down or speed up brain waves. Of all the different noise makers, music is perhaps the most practical and pervasive example of how noise can impact our lives.

Music is perhaps one of the most powerful forces around. No wonder people everywhere love it. In terms of our overall health, music can: affect heart rate, respiration, blood pressure, and body temperature; boost immunity (music literally can oxygenate cells); release endorphins (powerful natural stimulants); boost productivity; increase endurance; regulate stress-related hormones; improve and alter our mood; trigger memories, both good and bad; and much more.

In short, music is powerful. We should make it a priority to find what works for us in terms of overall health and well-being.

Music can increase our spatial reasoning and thus our IQ/ intellect, return lost memories, help cure addictions, heal brain injuries, and more.

According to anesthesiologists, for people listening to re- laxing, ambient music, the level of stress-related hormones in their blood declines significantly.

Now, the negative. It is proven that high levels of noise and noise pollution can cause health problems in humans. Some of the problems include stress, high blood pressure, issues related to the heart and blood vessels, hearing, insomnia, and the like. All of this of course directly affects sex life.

We process noise subconsciously, so even if we feel that we are "tuning out" noise, it still affects us harmfully in a subtle manner. It contributes to raising our blood pressure, increas- ing heart rate and so forth. Noise pollution has been linked to irritability and depression. The World Health Organiza- tion estimates that in Western Europe alone, over a million life years are lost annually due to traffic noise pollution.

CHAPTER 15

Absolute Sex

Sexual Techniques

The following sexual techniques, tips, and stages are all part of the entire process of experiencing screaming, simultaneous orgasms. They are a fundamental and intrinsic part of the package. If any of them are left out, it will be more challenging to experience screaming orgasms.

Non-Verbal Communication- NVC

There are some very practical techniques I will share with you. But I want to cover this one first, because it is so important and so neglected and misunderstood. This area is a little more intangible, subtle and elusive.

Non-verbal communication (NVC) is the unknown factor in all the sexual techniques out there. It is the X factor, the mysterious facet, the ethereal dynamic.

If you can develop effective non-verbal communication, your romantic and sexual life will have no limits. NVC is vital and critical to fulfilling, dynamic romantic and sexual relationships.

We would all agree that communication is perhaps the most important part of social interaction and romance. It is how we develop a relationship with someone. Communication is how we keep our current relationship strong and growing.

In fact, and please know that the following statement is very, very deep, yet seems so simple: Life is Communication.

Life is communication between the divine and the human; between humans; between humans and animals; and much, much more.

And check this out: some psychological studies have found that as much as 90% of communication is non-verbal.

Our NVC is so loud that other people often do not really hear what we say.

Who we are is in some ways as important if not more important than the actual words we say.

What are examples of non-verbal communication? Just some examples are: Body language, posture, facial expressions, eye contact, nonverbal elements in speech, voice tone, smiles (or lack thereof), hand gestures, touching (or lack thereof), proximity, clothing, hair styles and many more.

There are many, many aspects of NVC- and many that we do not even realize or aware of. The way someone walks and stands is NVC. The way someone talks is NVC. The way someone listens in NVC, and it is just as important as what they say and they way they talk.

The way someone takes care of him or herself is part of NVC. I am referring to health and fitness, personal hygiene, hair style and length, body hair and more.

In terms of romance and sex, NVC is an incredibly important factor.

When it comes to romance, a person's NVC may be the most important and misunderstood component.

If a guy can be himself and exhibit confidence and positive NVC through body language, speech tone, personal lifestyle choices and many other factors, women will naturally be attracted to him.

At the same time, if a guy can learn to read a woman's NVC, he will save a lot of time and hassle knowing who is interested in him and who to pursue- and who not to pursue.

Same with a woman. If she can harness the power of NVC, she will begin to attract the type of guy she wants and desires. And if she can learn to read guys and their NVC, she will know who to spend time with and who to avoid.

And the same applies to two lovers and their relationship. If they can learn to read each other's NVC, their relationship will grow deeper and stronger. If they learn to communicate non-verbally, they will move into deeper dimensions in their union.

If they can communicate non-verbally in their sexual relationship, they will experience a deeper and stronger sexual connection.

Some excellent resources are two books: The Definitive Book of Body Language by Barbara and Allan Pease and You Don't Say: Navigating Non Verbal Communication Between the Sexes, by Audrey Nelson and Susan Gollant.

Someone's personal lifestyle choices and habits are a major part of NVC. Some examples are: choices about make-up, perfume and cologne; clothing preferences; choices related to food, alcohol, tobacco and narcotics; choices about tattoos and body piercings; and so on.

Obviously, some choices can be turn-offs to some people. If someone has body odor, for example, that can be a real turn-off. It takes effort and planning to get into the right sexual "zones" that are primed for orgasms.

Flirting

Yes, flirting and having fun with your partner during the day is an important part of sex. Many people neglect this aspect of their sexual relationship.

Flirting builds excitement and energy and releases tension. It allows partners to connect in unique and fun ways.

Flirting and sex are about having fun. Keep it simple and fun. I have had clients enter new realms of connection in their relationship through the simple act of flirting. And many have come up with new ways to have fun flirting.

There are countless ways to flirt! It is an art, and people who develop their flirting skills have a great time. More importantly, they improve their sex life automatically. It is a great turn-on to both guys and girls.

Author Gloria Liven includes 101 ways to flirt on her great website Studiosoflove.com. Check it out. There are some really fun and effective ideas there.

Susan Rabin's book 101 Ways to Flirt: How To Get More Dates and Meet Your Mate is another great resource for flirting ideas.

Have fun! Remember that an important part of flirting and romance is NVC. This is so key. In fact, flirting is all about NVC. Learning positive, confident NVC is a key to effective flirting.

A key is that flirting can lead to fun, innocent and playful foreplay- and then sex- with your lover. Flirting does not stop at some point in time. It naturally can lead to great sex. It can all flow together.

Flirting allows a man and woman to read each other. Perhaps a guy flirts with his lover, only to find she may not be in the mood for sex. Or maybe she is. The art of flirting is a chance to engage in some NVC with your partner to read him or her.

There are a thousand simply ways to flirt. Leave notes, send simple cards, give a small gift, have inside jokes.

Phone Message apps and other smart phone communication apps are great ways to flirt and have fun with each other. The apps are great for private messages.

Textie, Textfree and Heywire are other messaging apps that allow users to text and message freely and economically.

Pillow Talk

This is a must! There is a saying, 'Life is communication.' And pillow talk is a great to create life in your relationship and your romance.

Pillow talk is the personal, intimate talk between two partners in bed (or anywhere, really) either after or before sex- or anytime! Do not limit the talk only to post-sex. It is a great way to connect with your partner and build intimacy.

The talk may lead to intimacy and sex, or it may not. It is a great time to simply connect and bond. It can be a time to unwind and get away from the pressures of the day. Partners usually keep the talk very simple and focus on positive, uplifting things. Do not bring up anything negative, such as work stress, family issues or financial issues. Avoid them like the plague!

And here is something that can help your relationship generally; it has helped many of my clients. Discuss those serious, stressful issues in a specific place in the home, at certain times and even in certain clothes. This strategy helps to keep them "separate" from the rest of your life.

For example, a couple has several major issues they need to talk about, related to: money, bills, a relationship issue (a husband wants some space to go out with friends one night a week, etc), a child rearing issue, etc.

The couple might consider discussing some of these issues on weekdays (let's say M or Tues), at about 6 pm before dinner, in the dining room that is not used very often. They talk, they communicate their feelings and thoughts, and then at about 6:30 they continue their day. The issues are "sequestered" and "left there" in the dining room after the talk.

Now, as they continue their week, the hope is that a majority of their talk and communication will be positive and have good vibes, especially pillow talk! In pillow talk, whether they are in their bedroom, the den, on the sofa watching a movie, in the kitchen, wherever, their communication is 100% positive, fun and affectionate. The serious issue talk is reserved for.....a certain day, time and place, and it is left there.

Foreplay

Foreplay is an essential and vital component of sex and screaming orgasms. It is part of the whole package. In one way, it is like the prelude or opening act.

But I want you to view all the steps flowing together. They are not "separate steps" that begin and end. This is a key to one of the main techniques I will share with you. For example, foreplay extends into the actual act of sexual intercourse. It is a gradual, slow process that builds and builds- and results in powerful, fulfilling, screaming orgasms.

Again, if someone skips foreplay, they can still have great sex, but they are missing out on having absolutely fantastic sex.

All the steps in this process flow together. Visualize them flowing together- general communication, flirting, foreplay, stimulation, arousal, intercourse and on.

We all know the basic foreplay techniques. And we know

the purpose: build arousal for both partners through sexual stimulation leading to sex.

Remember how important the sensation of touching is to women? This is when it really comes into play.

Some basic techniques are: kissing- all over the body, including the lips, face, neck, ears, shoulders, chest, breast area and more; French kissing, touching, caressing, massage, fondling, playing, undressing, lingerie and similar techniques.

Foreplay is an art, and it does take effort and time.

Many guys just want to go right to penetration. Remember, steps like foreplay are critical to building excitement and arousal- and having screaming orgasms.

Some keys with foreplay are having fun, being creative and thinking outside the box.

Teasing

Teasing is an essential part of the entire process leading to screaming orgasms. It is also an art.

It is a truly sexy way to build arousal and sexual energy in a woman. But so many men ignore and neglect teasing. They do not realize how powerful it is.

I cannot tell you how many men I've counseled who do not tap into the powerful technique of teasing.

And there are so many ways to tease, excite and tantalize a woman. There are an infinite number of ways! I encourage men to put on their creative hats and have a blast enticing their lover into new realms of sexual excitement.

There are so many creative ways to tease, I almost do not want to focus on specifics. I will at least pass along some general and specific ideas. And these apply to both men and women.

Go slow. Make real eye contact. Deliberately take your

time. Let suspense build. Perhaps acknowledge arousal (like an erection or stimulated nipples), but do not go there yet.

Massage. Utilize the powerful technique of massage in all its different forms. It can be a full massage with lotion. It can be a 30 second massage. Again, there are countless ways to incorporate massage into teasing.

Anchoring. Practice and learn the effective technique of anchoring, which involves association of the touch of a specific place on the body with a good feeling. This anchor (for example, on the shoulder or the upper back), when it is associated with the good feeling, can be utilized at any time to re-produce the positive sensation.

Take the anchoring to a higher level by associating your voice with the touch.

Both men and women can utilize anchoring on their partner. Many women have told me this technique has helped them develop confidence in their romantic life. They were able to put a practical technique into action and see results.

Visualize what might take place. Visualize undressing her or him. This will cause your sexual energy barometer to sky rocket.

Men and women get great results from visualization. Men get aroused with a strong erection. Women get wet in their genital area. It works.

Let tremendous sexual energy be released from you into your partner with every kiss, suck and breath. This phenomenon is powerful. Practice and develop this technique. Combine it with visualization to produce a potent sexual excitement tool.

This same skill applies to certain professional vocations.

Professional and career experts talk about how selling is a "transfer of energy" from one person to another. I understand what they mean. A salesperson is selling a product, but in a real sense they are selling in idea or a concept, and their passion for it makes a big different.

I think a step further is that the best selling is a controlled, reserved and discreet transfer of energy. Whether it is in sales, marketing, motivation or whatever, some people might overdo it and oversell. It comes across as cheesy and fake.

But the best sell is that confident, poised, centered and controlled transfer of energy and passion.

Similar techniques apply in romance and sex.

Note: I am just making a point here. I do not want to get career mixed up with sex. Some people have stressful careers and jobs, and they certainly do not want to associate their career with sex.

Then again, as we discussed earlier, every area affects every other area. A positive experience at work has a positive impact on your sex life. And vice-versa.

Mood and environment. Get the mood right in the room- appropriate lighting, light music, aromatherapy. Get the temp right. Perhaps enjoy a favorite beverage (regular or adult).

Slowly kiss and French kiss while caressing your lover's back and body.

Kiss and caress your lover all over- cheek, neck, ears, shoulders, arms, chest area, stomach, back.

Go near the breasts and then back away and go to other parts of the body. The stomach, hips, thighs, inner thighs, buttocks.

Then go back to the breasts, slowly and deliberately. Maybe go close to them a few times and back away. Tease and tantalize. Use your hands, fingers, mouth, tongue and lips. Do not touch the nipples yet.

Women can take the initiative and engage in similar teasing. Caress and fondle your lover's back, buttocks, hips and legs.

Gently rub his genitals. Let him know you notice his arousal and verbally give approval.

Be creative. Perhaps go back to the face, cheek, lips and neck. Slowly undress your lover. Let him or her slowly undress you.

At the right time, men, you can go to the nipples and have at it. Use your hands, fingers and mouth. Feel, caress and stroke them in countless different motions. Kiss, suck and gently bite them.

CHAPTER 16

Sex Positions

Sex Positions for Orgasm

The following sexual positions are ideal for sexual pleasure and for inducing orgasms. A key to experiencing orgasms regarding various positions is to keep it simple!

It might be exciting to swing from contraptions and chandeliers during sex, but the reality is that acrobatics and "advancements" in sex often distract from the pleasure.

The basic sex positions with slight variations are the most effective for reaching heights of pleasure and the ultimate height: orgasms.

Spooning

Spooning is when both partners are on their sides, with the man lying behind his partner and entering her vagina from behind. This technique concentrates on the front portion of the vagina or rectum, where most of the highly sensitive nerve endings are. It's a great position for relaxed, laid back stimulation, a unique position for a lazy summer afternoon-and highly arousing with great potential for orgasm.

Crisscross

Both partners lie down, with the man on his side and the woman on her back. She drapes her legs over his middle in a crisscross or "X" shape. In this position, both partners have full access to her genital area and clitoris, which is what most women need to reach a real orgasm.

Ankles and Legs High

Everyone may know about these positions but may not take advantage of them. When a woman's legs and ankles are lifted high, with her feet either on her lover's chest or over his shoulders, the man can enter her perhaps the deepest he possibly can. This depth often allows him to reach her G-spot, the highly sensitive in a woman. Experiment with the placement of her legs, ankles and feet to find out which position allows for which specific stimulation and the level of depth.

Reverse Cowgirl

This woman on top position is another all-time, top-of-the-list favorite for both men and women. While at times men and women prefer their partner to face them, giving them easy access to her breasts and allowing truly intimate kissing and french-kissing while making love and much more (!), the reverse cowgirl truly is a great orgasm position. Why? First, it allows for different vaginal sensations for the women. Next, and moreover, direct clitoral stimulation is easy to engage in, a key to for a woman reaching orgasm.

Slow Climb

In the missionary position, place a pillow under the woman's butt. The woman pulls her legs all the way up to her shoulders (as far as is comfortable), like she is bending in half. This position allows deeper penetration and allows him a very easy angle for penetration. It also allows him to reach and stimulate her G-spot. Consider this a primer for other positions as well. When G-spot stimulation builds arousal and increases sensitivity.

CAT- Coital Alignment Technique

While in the missionary, the guy moves about two inches forward (that is, slide two inches up), with his shoulders above hers, which aligns both of your pelvic bones. The woman puts her legs together between his, which are now outside her legs. This aligns his thrusting with her clitoris. The guy can rock and gradually bring her to climax. He can use her feet as a brace.

Down dog

Woman lies face down with her butt slightly up in air, allowing for penetration. Man can lie on her or use hands like he is doing a push-up. The face-down position can provide increased friction as he moves in and out. In addition, his thrusting can gently stimulate her clitoral area on the bed.

Legs Over Butt

Woman lies on her back, man is on his side. Woman places legs over his thighs and butt, and the man can now penetrate.

This is an easy position to maintain and is not as tiring as some positions. She can stimulate herself, or he can stimulate with his top hand.

Scissors

Man lies on his back with knees bent and feet on bed. The woman places on leg outside his waist and one leg between his legs. She can ride him and find the right spot to grind against his pubic bone, and she has complete control of the speed, depth and friction she experiences.

Reveal the Clit

During intercourse, the woman can use her first two fingers (in a V) to pull up the clitoral hood and mons pubis so that the clit can receive more stimulation during sex. This simply technique can be very effective.

Female Superior

In surveys, time and again the woman-on-top position is the male favorite. There is just something out of this world and mind-blowingly sexy, erotic, and just plain orgasmic about a his woman on top and the entire process: a man lying down or sitting in a chair; his woman climbing up and using her vagina in this unique way, sliding it onto this shaft and penis; and then the myriad of different ways she can send him to new heights of ecstasy.

Seated Lotus

He sits with legs crossed, Indian style. She straddles his waist and rides him in a variety of ways and styles. This position has great advantages. She can control all aspects of the intercourse, including the depth, speed, tempo, and pace of her movement as well as the angle and depth and more. He has access to her body, clit, and breasts. Both partners are facing each other, so it is very romantic and intimate.

Indian Stradle

A variation of the seated lotus. He sits with legs extended instead of crossed. Guys can experiment and see which variatons he and she likes. Fun experiment, right?

Reverse with Feet Flat

This is a twist On the woman-on-top position. The girl does a 180 and twists around on her guy's member, so that her back is facing him. Instead of reverse cowgirl, with feet outside his legs, she places both feet flat on the bed/floor, with feet together. There are two big benefits to this. With legs together, the fit is even tighter. It also allows for increased G-spot stimulation. Add in your own clit stimulation, and both of you will explode to new heights.

Edge of Table

She lies on table that is waist-high for the guy, with her butt at edge of table. Resting her legs on his shoulders or dangling them off the table, he has easy access to her body and can easily stimulate her clit. She can lift her butt and clench on is member, increasing the stimulation.

Male Superior

Missionary

Yeah, it may be the most basic position, but you would be surprised how versatile and stimulating it is. It has numerous variations as well. Utilize missionary to your advantage: let it lead to other erotic positions.

The X-Factor

A variation of the missionary, the X involves the guy rotating his body clockwise or counter-clockwise, allowing for different angles and depths of penetration.

The Pick Up

Standing up and facing each other, he picks her up, while she straddles his hips. He enters her, with the new position allowing deep and different penetration. Recommended for men with good upper body strength.

Side by side

The Armchair

In this position, he literally is her chair. He sits on the bed or floor, and she sits in his lap, facing the same direction he is facing. She rides him, controlling the depth, pace, and speed. At the same time, she can stimulate her clit, and he can play with her breasts. This is a great combo position, combining aspects of woman on top and doggie style. Keep in mind that this position is physically demanding for the guy.

Relaxed Bridge

This is a position for slower, relaxed sex and stimulation. It's a great position to combat fatigue. The woman lies on her back, with the man lying on his side and facing her. She places her legs over his body like a bridge. He has easy access to thrust, with both partners being able to rest at the same time. The stimulation increases, especially if the man also stimulates her breasts, zones, and clit manually.

CHAPTER 17

Passion Principle

Self-discovery is an important aspect of sexuality.

It's still amazes me how many women I counsel who have not learned about their sexual anatomy and genitals. A woman must know her genitals to experience great sex and orgasms. The more a woman knows and understands about her anatomy, the more knowledge and power she has for great sex. Looking at, being aware of, and exploring your sexual parts is a great way to advance sexually.

Perhaps the best way to gain this understanding is through masturbation. It is one of the best ways for a woman to find out what she likes. It is easy, free, and personal. Self-stimulation is a surefire way to move up to a higher level sexually. Studies and surveys show that a majority of women masturbate.

When a woman learns and knows what works for them, it is easier for her to show her partner what works. A practical technique is for partners to masturbate in front of each other; or to stimulate each other at the same time. This can spice up your sex life.

One of the best ways to learn is by using a mirror.

Make Orgasms More Powerful

1. Relax

A key to stronger orgasms is being able to relax during sex and when you reach climax and peak sensations. Some simple techniques to relax include:

vocalization and emoting; that is, freely expressing yourself verbally rather than keeping it inside;

pushing out pelvic muscles, similar to when you urinate;

spreading your toes

2. Visualize

Yes, this works. Visualize yourself having a massive powerful orgasm. Expect it. Get ready for it. Know it's going to happen. Talk about it with your partner. It's best if they expect and get ready for it as well.

Also, visualize the pleasure and response going from your head to your genital area. After all, orgasms occur in the genital area. But it starts in your mind as something you want. Literally visualize the orgasm moving from your brain to your groin.

3. Know what works for you and your lover

Find and learn what you and your partner like and don't like. Experiment. Try new things. Talk about it. Many couples tell me they find what works, and they stick with it.

A Simple Exercise Trick
to Make Orgasms More Powerful

The better physical shape you are in, the better your orgasms are. It's pretty simple. Orgasms are a physical and physiological response.

There are a lot of different physical tricks that can make orgasms more powerful.

The Pelvic, Thigh, and Penis Base Muscles

A program of tightening and releasing the pelvic, thigh, and PC/penis base muscles will greatly tone and strengthen this overall area, which will cause your orgasms to be much more powerful, extended, and releasing. For girls and guys, this is the same technique used to "hold back" urination. Try it. It works.

Tighten this area for five seconds and release. Do three to five reps. Do this every hour or two three times a day. If you are already in great physical shape, you may want to start out faster: hold for 10 seconds and do five to 10 reps every hour or three to five times per day. Do what works for you. This can of course be done anywhere, anytime. Have fun with this. Listen to your body. This technique is effective.

Spine Realignment

The entire spine is obviously a key to health. If someone has neck, back, or lower back issues, their health and their sex life are adversely affected. There's a simple way to keep the entire spine healthy.

Try this technique every 30 minutes or so, during the normal course of your day, while standing. Act like a wire is pulling the top of your head and the base of your spine in opposite directions. Gently but firmly do this: "stretch" your head up and the base of your spine toward the ground. Hold this for 10-12 seconds and release. You'll be amazed at how this can tone, strengthen, and release your spine, and how it will give you energy for sex.

Connecting

Something I constantly try to communicate to my clients is the wonderful truth of connecting.

Sex is about a lot of things. But perhaps one of the most important is that the physical and sexual realms are vehicles for two people to connect in a deeper and more profound way than merely the mental, intellectual, psychological, and so forth.

Remember we spoke about humans having three parts: spirit, soul, and body. The sexual realm actually, I believe, includes all three parts. This is why two people who have sex often get emotionally and psychologically connected and therefore have a deeper connection and more difficult time during a break-up.

When two people connect intellectually, for example, they are in the soul realm. When they connect spiritually, they are in the spirit realm.

When two people have an emotional connection, and they may be in both the soul and spirit realm. Then if they connect sexually in a real way (and not just "boning up"), they are now connecting in all three realms and are entering the deepest connection possible for humans.

Two people can have sex and only connect in the physical realm, which is very limited. This happens all the time. Two people simply have sex, without a connection, and while it might be pleasurable, overall they almost always would say it is an empty experience.

CHAPTER 18

The Female Genitalia

It is extremely important for both men and women, boys and girls, to have a full understanding of both genders' genitals. This is important for several reasons: reproduction, pleasure, and self-care. I feel it's important to start young people early in this process.

The female genitalia are more complicated. It is of course very important to know and understand the wonder and mystery of the vagina - at least attempt to.

When a woman knows the dynamics of her genitals – how they work, what she likes, etc. – she is more comfortable and therefore more able and equipped to have satisfying orgasms.

The same is true for men regarding the vagina. When a man understands the female genitalia, he is much more able to pleasure his partner.

This same process applies to men's genitals. If a woman knows how the male genitals function and what her partner likes, she is more able to satisfy him.

As Bull said in the movie *Bull Durham* (which I highly recommend), "a woman's pussy is like the Bermuda triangle. A man gets lost in there you'll never see him again." This statement can have various meanings. First, a man might get lost in pleasure and exploration. But he also might get lost because he does not understand the vagina and its various parts. So let's take a look.

Today, the "vagina" usually refers to the vagina and the vulva. However, technically, they are two separate organs, the vagina being internal and the vulva external.

External Genitals: Vulva, Labia, and Clitoris

The vulva comprises the external genital parts. It is the outer doorway to the uterus, or womb. It protects the opening with its "double door" of the labia majora and labia minora.

The vulva has three main functions: 1.) it protects the sexual organs and urinary opening from trauma and infection, 2.) it is vital for sexual stimulation and response, with the vulva's clitoris being the most sexually sensitive spot for women, and 3.) it and the perineum stretch during childbirth.

The vulva have rich nerve endings and provide pleasure when stimulated.

The vulva also contains the opening of the female urethra, where urine is passed. Both openings, the vagina and the urethra, are protected by the labia.

Labia majora are the outer lips of the vulva. They are the pads of fatty tissue that wrap around the vulva from the mons pubis to the perineum. The majora are usually covered with pubic hair and contain oil and sweat glands. Some experts believe the scent from the glands is sexually arousing.

Labia minora are the inner lips of the vulva. The minora contain thin stretches of tissue that protect the vagina, urethra, and clitoris. The appearance of the minora can vary, from tiny, thin lips that almost hide in the majora, to thick, protruding lips. The minoras are sensitive to touch. Rubbing them even through clothing can be highly arousing for a woman.

Mons pubis- also called the mons veneris, which in Latin means "hill of Venus" (the Roman goddess of love). This is the pad of fatty tissue that covers the pubic bone and is above the labia but below the abdomen. For some women, the mons is sexually sensitive. It protects the pubic bone during intercourse.

Clitoris- ah, the legendary clit. It needs no introduction.

The clit only exists on the female and is the only body part that exists solely for pleasure.

The clitoris is a complex organ and structure, with both internal and external features. It is very interesting to note that the "glans clitoridis" is anatomically shaped like the penis and actually becomes very slightly erect when stimulated correctly.

The head of the clit is roughly the size of a pea (sometimes smaller or bigger.) At the base on the pubic mound, the clitoral hood covers the head (clitoral glans.)

The clitoral crura are the "legs" (crura literally translates to "legs) that are shaped like an inverted "V" below the clitoral head. The crura, like the rest of the clitoris, fill with blood during the excitement phase. The cruras are near the clitoral bulbs.

The clitoral bulb, also called the vestibular bulb, is erectile tissue that is an internal part of the clitoris. The bulb is also called the bulb of vestibule. During excitement, the bulbs fill with blood, causing the vaginal opening to be constricted, causing the vulva to expand outward. The blood is released during orgasm. If no orgasm, the blood is released gradually.

The vulval vestibule is the part of the vulva between the labia minora where the vaginal opening and the urethral opening are. The vestibule contains the Skene's gland and the Bartholin's gland.

The hymen is the thin tissue or membrane that covers the vaginal opening. A slang term for the hymen is the "cherry." The hymen usually breaks during a woman's first time of intercourse, and sometimes it "pops." The hymen is completely lost during childbirth. All of this is natural and does not affect a woman's health or periods.

Internal Genitals: Vagina, Uterus, Ovaries, and G-Spot

The vagina is the fibromuscular tract that extends from the cervix to the outer opening. It leads internally to the uterus, or womb, and ends at the cervix.

The average vagina, unaroused, is about three inches long. When aroused and during sexual activity, the vagina can extend in length as long as necessary to receive the penis.

The three inches may seem short, but during sex the cervix will extend upward and the fornix might also extend upwards in order to receive the penis. After sex, the vagina will contract, allowing the cervix to rest inside the cervix, creating a shape like a bowl, which is perfect for the pooling of semen.

The Bartholin's gland and the hyman glands produce, located on either side of the vaginal opening, produce lubricating fluid to keep the labia and the length of the vaginal canal moist for sex.

The vagina is lined with mucous membrane. It includes two vault-like structures sic, the anterior and posterior fornix. The cervix protrudes into the vagina, and through a tiny hole called the os, sperm travel to the female reproductive organs.

The inner mould of the vagina creates friction and stimulation for the penis during intercourse.

The average length of an unaroused vagina is about 2.5 to

3 inches. During arousal, the vagina expands in both length and width. The length reaches about 4 inches.

Glands and the membrane of the vaginal wall produce lubrication and moisture near the vaginal opening and the cervix, especially during sexual arousal and intercourse.

The vaginal rugae is the series of ridges resulting from the folding of the wall of the outer third of the vagina. The rugae provide increase surface for stretching and extension.

The outer one-third of the vagina has over 90% of the nerve endings of the entire vagina and is therefore much more sensitive to stimulation than the inner vaginal tract.

CHAPTER 19

Sexual Relationship Needs

There is a time and place for everything.

Regarding sex, there is a time for the routine . . . and a time for the new.

By routine, I mean: if it works, do it! If two partners find a sexual release that works, such as The Technique explained in this book, keep doing it.

At the same time, couples need new sexual experiences. It might mean new romantic experiences, in new places, with new and different sexual positions.

Needs in a Sexual Relationship

1. Certainty: assurance you can avoid pain and gain pleasure
2. Uncertainty/Variety: the need for the unknown, change, new stimuli
3. Significance: feeling unique, important, special or needed
4. Connection/Love: a strong feeling of closeness or union with someone or something
5. Growth: an expansion of capacity, capability or under-

standing

6. Contribution: a sense of service and focus on helping, giving to and supporting others

Security... knowing that financially you will be okay no matter what happens

Confidence... being able to press ahead with your life with a strong degree of positivity

Choice... not feeling trapped or on the treadmill of life; the ability to choose brings a sense of freedom

Faith... for some it is religion and for others it may be a strong belief in a moral code

Legacy... having a pride in what you have created and/or what you stand for

Making a difference... in whatever you are doing, helping others, not being introspective

Sense of belonging/love... We need a strong feeling of connection and to feel loved by family and friends

Stimulus... Something to get excited about; hobbies and experiences being a prime example

Influencing... being able to influence matters in a positive way brings empowerment

Variety... this is so important; "all work and no play makes Jack a dull boy" as the saying goes

CHAPTER 20

Marriage

Two is better than one.

Everything is more fun with someone else.

A partnership with someone you love . . . only one thing is greater than this: a partnership with God.

Marriage is wonderful. Why? It's simple: God created it.

And God created sex for numerous reasons. One of the main ones is that sex a primary part of the physical bond between a man and wife.

When a couple is united physically and sexually, it strengthens and confirms their overall deeper relationship: their emotional, psychological, even metaphysical bond.

When a couple breaks that sexual bond, such as if a partner cheats and/or has an affair, etc., it of course greatly damages their relationship.

No worries though. Even if cheating has occurred, a couple can be healed and restored. God can heal them and restore their marriage.

All men and women are seeking a deep emotional live. This deep love is found when both partners are united in spirit, soul and body.

Bibliography and Recommended Reading

I Love Female Orgasm: An Extraordinary Orgasm Guide, Dorian Solot and Marshall Miller

The Passion Prescription, Laura Berman

The Illustrated Guide to Extended Massive Orgasm, Steve and Vera Bodansky

How to Satisfy a Woman Every Time...and Have Her Beg for More!, Naura Hayden

About the Author

Sarah Taylor is a couples and sex therapist. Her goal is to help people discover God's gift of sex in a marriage.

www.ingramcontent.com/pod-product-compliance
Lightning Source LLC
Chambersburg PA
CBHW072207090426
42740CB00012B/2426